THE ESSENTIAL MARX

THE ESSENTIAL MARX

Paul Strathern

TED SMART

This edition published in Great Britain in 2002 by
Virgin Books Ltd
Thames Wharf Studios
Rainville Road
London
W6 9HA

First published in the USA in 2001 as *Marx in 90 Minutes* by Ivan R Dee

A catalogue record for this book is available from the British Library.

This book produced for The Book People Ltd,
Hall Wood Avenue, Haydock, St Helens, WA11 9UL

ISBN 0 7535 0954 7

Typeset by TW Typesetting, Plymouth, Devon
Printed and bound in Great Britain by
Clays Ltd, St Ives PLC

CONTENTS

INTRODUCTION 1

MARX'S LIFE AND WORKS 3

AFTERWORD 40

FROM MARX'S WRITINGS 42

CHRONOLOGY OF SIGNIFICANT PHILOSOPHICAL DATES 47

CHRONOLOGY OF MARX'S LIFE AND TIMES 50

RECOMMENDED READING 53

INDEX 55

INTRODUCTION

In 1848, the year that Karl Marx published the first *Communist Manifesto*, there were revolutionary disturbances throughout Europe, from Sicily to Warsaw. In Paris the uprising led to the fall of the Orléans monarchy; in Vienna the reactionary and repressive chancellor Metternich was forced to flee in disguise, 'like a criminal'. France and the Austro-Hungarian Empire were the two major powers on the continental mainland. It looked as if Europe was on the brink. But the forces of reaction eventually won the day, and their retribution was awesome. The scene in Dresden described by Clara Schumann (wife of the composer) was typical:

'They shot down every insurgent they could find, and our landlady told us later that her brother, who owns the Golden Stag in Scheffelgasse, was made to stand and watch while the soldiers shot one after another twenty-six students they found in a room there. Then it is said they hurled men into the street by the dozen from the third and fourth floors. It is horrible to have to go through these things! This is how men have to fight for their little bit of freedom! When will the time come when all men have equal rights?'

Marx proposed communism as the answer. The twentieth-century experience has taught us in no uncertain terms that it does not work. Yet several of Marx's most perceptive criticisms of capitalism remain unanswered. The questions of social justice which he raised – pressing and crucial at the time – remain with us. The cheek-by-jowl existence of luxury and pitiless destitution that can be found today in Bombay and São Paulo would be all too recognisable to the Marx who walked the streets of Dickensian London. Even in the heartlands of twenty-first-century affluence created by capitalism, its 'contradictions' are still evident in the urban ghettos of New York and Los Angeles, the economic wastelands of northeast England, and the slums of Naples. Capitalism has become *the* worldwide success story, but at cost. In Marx's time, this cost was beginning to appear unbearable.

MARX'S LIFE AND WORKS

Karl Marx was born in the German provincial city of Trier on 5 May 1818. Trier is just six miles from the Luxembourg border, on the Mosel River, which is renowned for its vineyards. Its proximity to the border and its love of wine make Trier an easy-going cosmopolitan spot, factors which were to have a significant influence on Marx.

Like so many ardent revolutionaries, Marx was brought up amidst comfortable bourgeois surroundings. His father, Hirschel, was a successful local lawyer who also owned a couple of small vineyards; and one of Karl's uncles went on to found the Dutch industrial giant Philips. Although descended from a line of rabbis, Hirschel Marx was not religious. Like many German Jews during this period – such as the composer Felix Mendelssohn and the poet Heinrich Heine – he converted to Christianity. This was largely a formality, enabling him to assimilate more easily into German middle-class society. Hirschel (who now became Heinrich) Marx had already enthusiastically embraced European culture. His favourite authors were Kant and Voltaire: a characteristic blend of German profundity and French subversive wit. Germany was in the process of becoming a unified nation state, and in 1815 the Rhineland provinces had been taken over by Prussia.

The new Prussian rulers were deemed autocratic and oppressive by the more liberal locals. Karl's father joined a political club that pressed for the Prussian state to adopt a constitution, which would enshrine the rights of its citizens.

Few details of Karl's childhood have come down to us, apart from his so-called habit of forcing his sisters to eat mud pies. This sounds like a legend based upon a single incident: weeping muddy-lipped girls, outraged mother, skulking Karl, etc. Needless to say, commentators have exploited its metaphorical implications to the full – this is what the mature Karl did to us all, and so forth. By the time he went to nearby Bonn University at the age of seventeen, Karl was already an avid imbiber of books and wine, dividing his time equally between the library and the taverns. During some riotous activity in the latter he managed to provoke a local officer cadet into challenging him to a duel, and was lucky to emerge from this episode with nothing more serious than a traditional duelling scar. Karl was never the athletic type and even managed to evade military service on health grounds (aided by a somewhat suspect doctor's report).

A year later Marx transferred to the University of Berlin, ostensibly to continue his law studies. But by now he had discovered philosophy, and all else paled into insignificance. Berlin was the capital of Prussia, far from the wine-loving Rhineland, and here student life was a much more serious matter. This was where the great Hegel had been professor of philosophy, becoming almost the official philosophical apologist for the Prussian state. But Hegel had died five years earlier, and a wide range of his followers had by now developed his ideas in a wide range of directions. Hegel's vast idealistic philosophical system had proved open to many contradictory interpretations, several of which were anything but sympathetic to the repressive Prussian state and all it stood for.

Marx dutifully attended the official lectures on Hegel's philosophy but claimed that he eventually fell ill 'from intense vexation at having to make an idol of a view I detested'. Ironically, Hegel proved to be one of the main influences on Marx's philosophy. But it was the dynamics and scope of this philosophy, rather than its actual content, that appealed to Marx.

Hegel's philosophy viewed the world and all history in terms of a vast, all-embracing, ever-evolving system. This evolution grew out of the struggle between contradictions, and worked in a dialectical fashion. Each notion implied and generated the notion of its contradiction. For instance, the very notion of 'being' implied the notion of 'nonbeing', or nothingness. These two opposites (the thesis and its antithesis) then came together to form their synthesis, which was 'becoming'. In Hegel's all-embracing dialectical system, this synthesis then became a new thesis, which in its turn developed its own antithesis, and so on. This dynamic system moved through all ideas, all history, and all phenomena – up to the highest level of Absolute Spirit reflecting upon itself, which is the totality of all that exists.

More specifically, Hegel's philosophy of history insisted that the evolution of laws and government institutions in a society reflected the ethos and character of the people who made up that society. This may seem obvious to anyone who is used to living in a more liberal society, but it was far from obvious 150 years ago in the repressive, bureaucratic Prussian state. Hegel insisted that there was a dialectical link between the state and its citizens. This dialectic assumed both a logical and an organic aspect. The evolving structure of the state and the evolving traditions of its people were part and parcel of the same thing.

Hegel's immensely prolix and complex philosophy appeared at an opportune historical moment. Its idealism, its insistence that all was moving towards the Absolute Spirit, filled the spiritual vacuum left by a growing disillusion with religion. It was Hegel who originally pronounced 'God is dead' in 1827, not his firebrand successor Nietzsche, who is usually associated with this saying. Hegel was referring here to the more limited Christian idea of God, which would be superseded by the Absolute Spirit. Even so, his remark was highly blasphemous. Yet it was buried deep in the obfuscation of his all but unreadable work, and passed largely unnoticed. As a result, his philosophy appeared essentially conservative to the Prussian authorities. Its emphasis on a vast hierarchical system seemed like the absolute dream of a bureaucratic state. It was Hegel's insistence on the spiritual, his religiosity, and the repressive conservatism of his system that made Marx sick.

Another major influence on Marx's intellectual development at this juncture was the German humanist philosopher and moralist Ludwig Feuerbach, who was born in 1804 and had originally studied theology. In his early twenties Feuerbach had abandoned theology in favour of studying under Hegel in Berlin. But by the time Feuerbach published his major works, he had progressed far beyond the orthodox theology and orthodox Hegelianism of his earlier years. According to Feuerbach, Christianity had nothing to do with humanity's relation to God. This religion, like all religions, covertly involved the relation between humanity and its own essential nature. The attributes of God were nothing more or less than the projected attributes of humanity. Our so-called knowledge of God was in fact no more than knowledge about ourselves and our own nature. For Hegel, the pinnacle of his system had been God – in the form of Absolute Spirit reflecting upon itself. Feuerbach accepted this structure, and even its dynamic, but interpreted it from a humanistic viewpoint. Absolute Spirit reflecting upon itself was nothing more or less than humanity's own self-consciousness – man's consciousness of his own essential nature, his understanding of his substantive self. What for Hegel had been idealistic and spiritual, became for Feuerbach humanistic and *materialistic*. There was no 'spirit' involved. As we shall see, these ideas had a profound effect on Marx, though he did not swallow them whole. Ironically (and tellingly), Marx accepted the materialism of Feuerbach's ideas but criticised their lack of Hegelianism. Feuerbach's ideas were fine as they stood, but they lacked all dialectical and historical perspective. History, society, humanity itself (or its consciousness of itself in the form of God) were not changeless. They all *evolved*. They developed dialectically: the original idea generated its own self-contradiction, which was then resolved in a synthesis of these contradictions.

The overwhelming influence of Hegel, together with the vague ambiguities of his idealism, enabled his followers to develop his thought in all directions. The original thesis of Prussian conservatism soon generated its antithesis in the form of those who called themselves the Left Hegelians. Prominent among these was the Bavarian thinker Max Stirner, who had also attended Hegel's lectures in Berlin. Stirner's ideas were so extreme that they would later provide a philosophical backing for the anarchist movement. There was no denying the revolutionary implications of his extreme egoism. For Stirner, consciousness created reality: the individual ego was responsible for his world. Such things as social class, the masses, the state and even humanity itself had no objective reality. Once again, Marx would grasp the subtlety of these ideas and then reverse them. He was impressed by Stirner's insight into the profound relationship between consciousness and socio-historical reality. But for Marx it would be consciousness itself that was in fact created by these external material circumstances, not the other way around.

Marx now began developing his own philosophy, which attempted to combine these seminal ideas into a thoroughgoing materialism driven by dialectical forces. His aim was to 'stand Hegel on his head'. But Marx's youthful passion translated such ideas into heroic form. His doctoral thesis extolled Prometheus, the ancient Greek hero who stole fire from the gods and brought it down to humanity. For his punishment, Prometheus was chained to a rock in the Caucasus, where an eagle returned each day to peck out his ever-renewing liver. Marx would continue to identify with Prometheus throughout his life; this ancient Greek hero provides an uncanny metaphor for the fate of Marx and his ideas. The Greek translation of Prometheus means 'he who sees, or thinks, the future'.

When Marx left the University of Berlin he had high hopes of taking up a post at a minor German university. Unfortunately, Friedrich Wilhelm IV had now become kaiser of Prussia, and his reign ushered in a new reactionary era. Left Hegelians, and all those associated with this development of Hegel's thought, were dismissed from the state-controlled universities.

After searching somewhat haphazardly for a job, Marx found a position as a journalist, working for the newly founded *Rheinische Zeitung* (*Rhineland Times*), a liberal newspaper based in Cologne. Despite the appallingly prolix style he had picked up from Hegel, Marx turned out to be an excellent journalist. Theory may have inspired him to jargon, but practice inspired him to coin ringing phrases that would remain typical of his writing throughout his life.

Marx was so successful as a journalist that by the end of his first year in the job he had been promoted to editor. The idealistic, hard-drinking, hard-working boss was highly popular with his idealistic, hard-drinking, hard-working young staff, who nicknamed him the 'Moor' because of his swarthy bearded features. The *Rheinische Zeitung* quickly became a thorn in the side of the Prussian authorities and its circulation trebled, making it the highest-circulation paper in Prussia. Marx's social and political relationships now took a dialectical course, one that remained characteristic throughout his life. Having attacked the authorities, he proceeded to lambast the liberal opposition for its ineffectiveness. Next he launched into his left-wing staff, theoretical revolutionaries to a man, dismissing the whole idea of revolution as an impractical pipe dream which simply hadn't been thought through properly. Despite such sentiments, in 1843 the *Rheinische Zeitung* was closed down by the authorities.

In his growing dialectical fashion, Marx now took two contradictory actions in quick succession. First he decided to settle down and marry. Then he decided to abandon his homeland and move into exile. The woman he married was his childhood sweetheart. Jenny von Westphalen was widely reckoned to be 'the most beautiful girl in Trier', the scion of a local aristocratic family with powerful political connections. (Her father held a senior post in the government administration, and her older brother would become an extremely repressive minister of the interior in the Prussian government.) What on earth did the enchanting Jenny see in this scruffy young Jewish hell-raiser, who was even four years her junior? The fact is, Jenny was bored to death with life as a provincial social princess. She was highly intelligent, well read, and longed for a life away from the stifling upper-class circuit in Trier. Marrying the penniless Karl certainly brought her this, though perhaps not in the manner she had foreseen. But this was a love match on both sides. Through all their vicissitudes, Jenny and Karl remained profoundly attached to each other.

After marrying his aristocratic sweetheart, Marx carried her off to Paris. Now regarded as the revolutionary centre of Europe, Paris had already staged revolutions in 1789 (the French Revolution) and 1830 (the revolution that overthrew the restored monarchy). The city contained all kinds of left-wing political groups. Marx's ideas had evidently undergone still another dialectical transformation since his last days on the *Rheinische Zeitung*. He now believed that revolution *was* the answer, and soon became a member of the fledgling Communists. But how could the revolution come about? First, a thoroughgoing intellectual programme would have to be worked out. And if politics was to change, then so would economics. Marx began an intensive study of the founding father of economics, the Scotsman Adam Smith, and his successor, the Englishman David Ricardo. At the same time he began forging a philosophical basis for his thinking, in the form of his own epistemology. What are the grounds for our knowledge of the world? How do we know what we know, and how do we know if it is true?

Marx's epistemology is one of the weaker and less original aspects of his thought, but it is important for two reasons. It is the strictly philosophical basis of the great ideas to come, and its dynamic character echoes through all of Marx's systematic thought. As we have seen, he had transformed his influences to the point where they could blend to become an exclusively materialist philosophy. In line with this, he wished to base all knowledge on strictly scientific premises.

For Marx, our knowledge began in our experience – our sensations and perceptions – of the material world. But Marx's materialism differed significantly from that of his predecessors. Earlier materialists tended to view sensation and perception in passive terms. Light strikes our eyes, we feel heat, we hear a sound. Our perception of such sights and sounds in no way changes them: they are things that affect us. For Marx, on the other hand, such perception was an interaction between us, the subject, and the material object. This object (the world around us) becomes transformed in the process of being known. Our perception does not discover the truth of the world, just its appearance. Thus our knowledge too cannot be the truth. Instead, our knowledge consists of practical methods by which we can manipulate and gain control over the natural world. Our knowledge of the world is not passive, it is purposive. It is a two-way process – active and reactive – in line with the dialectic.

The synthesis of scientific knowledge we thus gain enables us to impose patterns of order and to manipulate or anticipate the workings of nature. This process does not arrive at the truth, as it is usually conceived. 'The question of whether objective truth can be attributed to human thought has nothing to do with theory, it is a purely practical question. The truth is the reality and power of thought, which can only be demonstrated in practice.' This leads Marx to his famous conclusion: 'Philosophers have previously only interpreted the world, but the real task is to *change* it.'

Much has been made of this statement. Taken as a philosophical *attitude*, it would seem to invalidate its author as a philosopher altogether – advocating as it does the abandonment of philosophy in favour of political action. His famous remark is thus open to all the *philosophical* objections lodged against it. But if it is seen in the light of his epistemology – an interactive process – it *does* have philosophical value. He is making a profound point. There is no such thing as objective truth. We learn about how the world works in order to use it, to live in it. Unfortunately, even in its original context Marx appears to have wanted to have it both ways.

In order to support himself in Paris, Marx secured an appointment as editor of the *German-French Yearbook*. Through this magazine he met a like-minded fellow contributor named Friedrich Engels, whose father owned cotton mills in the Rhineland and one in Manchester, England. The 23-year-old Engels had been working for the family business in Manchester for two years. In his spare time, however, he devoted himself to pursuing his revolutionary ideals, meeting Chartists and followers of Robert Owen as well as attending Communist meetings. Engels' dichotomies, unlike Marx's, were lived on the surface. A rebel at home, he nonetheless joined the family firm. Despite being a high-school dropout at seventeen, he went on to learn more than a smattering of twenty-four languages. Although he functioned as a respectable businessman and member of the cotton exchange in Manchester, he also lived quite openly with his working-class girlfriend, an illiterate Irish redhead named Mary Burns. It was Mary who led him through the Irish slums off Oxford Road, dangerous areas for all but their inhabitants. During the course of these visits Engels encountered the scenes that appeared in his ground-breaking work *The Condition of the Working Class in England*:

'Masses of refuse, offal, and sickening filth lie among standing pools in all directions; the atmosphere is poisoned by the effluvia from these, and laden and darkened by the smoke of a dozen tall factory chimneys. A horde of ragged women and children swarm about here, as filthy as the swine that thrive upon the garbage heaps and in the puddles . . . The race that lives in these ruinous cottages, behind broken windows . . . or in dark wet cellars, in measureless filth and stench . . . must really have reached the lowest stage of humanity . . . In each of these dens, containing at most two rooms, a garret and perhaps a cellar, on the average twenty human beings live.'

Amazingly, this was in the year or so *before* the Irish potato famine, when a million would die and many more would be forced to emigrate, spilling into such 'Little Irelands' all over Britain and North America. Yet when Engels walked with a fellow businessman and pointed out how these slums were a disgrace to Manchester, his colleague merely listened politely and then remarked to him on parting: 'And yet there is a great deal of money made here. Good morning, Sir!'

Engels had briefly met Marx when he was editor of the *Rheinische Zeitung*, but on that occasion neither had been impressed. Not until Engels began submitting articles for the *German-French Yearbook* did Marx recognise a true kindred spirit. The second time they met, Engels was enjoying a brief visit to Paris on his roundabout way home for a holiday. The Communist *bon viveur* and the grubby, cheroot-smoking journalist soon found they had much more in common than their large beards. During Engels' ten-day visit, the two of them struck up an immediate and profound rapport that would last a lifetime. Engels was the only friend with whom Marx never quarrelled. For his part, Engels worshipped Marx – the word is hardly too strong. He would devote much of his time and money in support of his hero-friend, to say nothing of the emotional and physical energy involved in this exacting task.

Although Marx was married and now had a baby daughter, he was still living the precarious attic life of a poor student. This too remained a permanent feature of Marx's life. As we shall see, it was due to something more than mere financial necessity. The lack of respectability or social responsibility appears to have fulfilled some unresolved psychological need. Marx remained poor for the rest of his life, yet it was never working-class poverty, with the accompanying extreme squalor and despair, such as Engels had witnessed in Manchester. Marx's poverty was always more that of the perennial student fallen on hard times – often extremely hard times, but recognisably that of the improvident 'gent'.

Marx and Engels soon began using the *German-French Yearbook* as a mouthpiece for their radical ideas, which in this way began circulating in Germany. The Prussian authorities soon began seizing copies of the magazine and put pressure on the French government to restrain Marx. As a result the magazine was closed down and Marx was expelled from France. Rather than return to Germany, he departed for Belgium, which had become independent just fourteen years earlier, and took up residence in Brussels. The impecunious Marx family was increased to four when Jenny gave birth to a son.

Engels followed Marx to Brussels, where they both joined the newly formed Communist League.

In recognition of their journalistic prowess, Marx and Engels were given the task of writing a manifesto for the League. This is the origin of the first *Manifesto of the Communist Party*. From the very beginning it was something of a misnomer. There was no Communist party – the Communist League was merely one of several groups that referred to themselves as Communists. Likewise, the idea of producing a manifesto was not to proclaim Communist policy but to establish precisely what that policy was! Marx and Engels were expected to take the various woolly and disparate ideas that constituted communism, and hammer them into some hard and fast definitive shape. This they would succeed in doing beyond the wildest dreams of their sponsors. The *Communist Manifesto* (as it is now more popularly known) eventually became one of the greatest worldwide best-sellers in the history of printing, along with the Bible and Shakespeare. There is no doubting that this forty-page document is *the* masterpiece of its kind.

Its opening is suitably dramatic: 'A spectre is haunting Europe – the spectre of communism.' In an early draft, Engels defined communism as 'the doctrine of the conditions for the emancipation of the proletariat . . . that class of society which procures its means of livelihood entirely and solely from the sale of its labour'. This would be achieved 'by the elimination of private property and its replacement by community of property'. According to Marx, whose ringing phrases dominate the document, 'The history of all hitherto existing society is the history of class struggles.' This had passed from the slave era through the feudal era to modern bourgeois society, where capitalists were able to dominate the proletariat because they owned the means of production, such as the machinery and the factories.

Surprisingly, Marx was quite ready to admit the unparalleled achievements of the bourgeois age: 'It has been the first to show what man's activity can bring about. It has accomplished wonders far surpassing the Egyptian pyramids, Roman aqueducts and Gothic cathedrals; it has conducted expeditions that put in the shade all former Exoduses of nations and crusades.' *But* – and here comes the full weight of Marx's analysis: 'It has pitilessly torn asunder the motley feudal ties that bound man to his "natural superiors", and has left remaining no other nexus between man and man than naked self-interest, than callous "cash payment". It has drowned the most heavenly ecstasies of religious fervour, of chivalrous enthusiasm, of philistine sentimentalism, in the icy water of egotistical calculation. It has resolved personal worth into exchange value, and in place of the numberless incontestable chartered freedoms has set up that single, unscrupulous freedom – Free Trade.' The human richness of mediaeval life (such as still lingered in preindustrial places like Trier) had given way to the industrial urban nightmare (such as could be witnessed from student attic windows in Berlin and Paris). Humanity had been dehumanised. Individual freedoms had been harnessed to free trade – the very factor which, according to Adam Smith, allowed the 'invisible hand' of the market to do its work, providing benefit for all.

Here for the first time was a trenchant analysis that was diametrically opposed to classical economics. The victory of the proletariat would bring about the first classless society. The market, free trade – these worked for the benefit of the capitalist, at the expense of the proletariat, who were simply exploited. There was no point in reform; the only answer lay in the overthrow of capitalism.

Despite this argument, in the *Manifesto* Marx does offer a list of reforms for capitalism. Those such as the progressive income tax, the abolition of child labour, and free education for all children we now accept as the norm. Others such as the abolition of private property and the establishment of a state monopoly in banking, communications, transport and all means of production, have been tried. The attempts to establish such utopian projects have forcefully brought home the actual meaning of the word utopia (which derives from the ancient Greek *ou*, meaning no, and *topos*, place). There is also a further recommendation by Marx, which often escapes comment: 'Confiscation of the property of all emigrants and rebels.' An odd suggestion, coming from an emigrant rebel – but since Marx seldom had any property, its author would presumably have remained unaffected by this Draconian measure.

The *Manifesto* ends with its celebrated call to arms:

'Communists disdain to conceal their views and aims. They openly declare that their ends can be attained only by the forcible overthrow of all existing social conditions. Let the ruling classes tremble at a Communist revolution. The proletariat have nothing to lose but their chains. They have a world to win.

'WORKERS OF THE WORLD, UNITE!'

Marx put the finishing touches to the *Manifesto* in January 1848. Although it was not circulated with sufficient speed or in sufficient numbers to have an immediate effect, there is no doubt that Marx caught the mood of the times. 1848 was to be the 'year of the revolutions' throughout Europe. In January a local revolution was sparked off in Sicily, the following month saw one in Paris, then it spread to Germany, the rest of Italy . . . The revolutionaries were not the only ones to think that bourgeois European civilisation was coming to an end.

Yet once again Marx went his own dialectical way. Encouraged by Engels, he astonished the Communist League by turning his back on the cause. The two of them left Belgium and returned to the Rhineland, where Marx accepted the post of editor of a resurrected *Neue Rheinische Zeitung*. To the amazement of his friends, Marx now began writing articles denouncing the revolution. In Marx's view, it was all a mistake. Instead, the working class should collaborate with the democratic bourgeoisie if anything worthwhile was to be achieved. This unexpected dialectical shift was to be short-lived, soon generating its own dialectical conclusion.

In September 1848, Kaiser Friedrich Wilhelm IV dissolved the Prussian Assembly in Berlin.This was too much for Marx, who immediately advocated armed resistance to such a suspension of democratic rights. He was arrested but put on a bravura performance at his trial. He told the jurors that he hadn't been advocating revolution, merely a defence of the realm. The king himself had been guilty of revolution. Such was the popular feeling of the moment that Marx was unanimously acquitted, and even thanked by the jury, amidst a cheering courtroom.

Meanwhile the fearful bourgeois backers of the *Neue Rheinische Zeitung* had withdrawn their support, but Marx managed to put out a final issue. This was printed in bright red ink, with Marx announcing in his editorial that his 'last word everywhere and always will be: *emancipation of the working class!*' The edition caused the expected uproar, and Marx was deported.

In August 1849, Marx arrived all but penniless in London, accompanied by his family, which had now increased to three small children, with Jenny pregnant once more. In a show of solidarity, he and Engels rejoined the Communist League, whose international headquarters was in London. For almost a year after their arrival in the city, the Marx family lived a hand-to-mouth existence. They moved from one cheap lodging to another in the shabbier back streets around Leicester Square favoured by many continental political exiles. That same year Jenny Marx gave birth to her fourth child, another son. Soon after this the family were evicted onto the street, along with their few sticks of furniture, for nonpayment of rent. They were rescued by the charity of a fellow exile, but by the end of the year Marx's infant son had died.

More lasting charity was now provided by Engels, who had given up his attempt to become a journalist. He had gone back to work for his father's factory in Manchester, at least in part so that he could support Marx. At the end of 1850, Marx and his family found more settled lodgings in two rooms on the top floor of 28 Dean Street in Soho. This was the beginning of Marx's decade-long period of oblivion – a time of spiritual and political isolation, supported by hand-outs from Engels, who was exiled two hundred miles away in Manchester.

The Communist League was Marx's only consolation. His charismatic and genuinely endearing personality, along with his daunting and far-ranging intellect, made him a natural leader. But his supreme political skills were best adapted to small groups, such as the newspaper office and the committee room. He had to dominate: he disliked appearing at public meetings or encountering intellectual peers who might cross swords with him. Marx found himself unable to dominate the Communist League, which soon fell apart, both in England and Germany, amidst a welter of bickering and recriminations – mostly inspired by clashes of personality masquerading as irreconcilable differences of policy. Marx's house in Dean Street was kept under permanent surveillance by Prussian police spies. He and Engels even wrote a joint letter to the *Spectator*, the best-known magazine in London, complaining 'the doors of the houses where we live are closely watched by individuals of a more than doubtful look, who take down their notes very coolly every time one enters the house or leaves it; we cannot make a single step without being followed by them wherever we go.' Somehow one of these spies even managed to gain entry into Marx's home, leaving us the most intimate picture we have of him during this period:

'As soon as you enter his room, your eyes are so dimmed by coal smoke and tobacco fumes that it is as if you are blundering into a cave . . . Everything is so dirty, and the place so full of dust, that even sitting down is a hazardous undertaking. The chair on which one sits has only three legs, the only whole chairs being used by the children to play and prepare food . . . Besides being a poor host, Marx is also a completely disorganised and cynical person. He leads the existence of a genuine bohemian intellectual. He very seldom washes himself, combs his hair, or changes his clothes. He also enjoys getting drunk. Sometimes he is idle for days on end, but he will work day and night with tireless endurance when he has a lot of work to do. He follows no routine when it comes to getting up or going to sleep. Frequently he stays up all night; then he lies down fully clothed on the sofa at noon, and sleeps until evening, oblivious to whoever passes in and out of the room.'

In all fairness, this chaotic regime must in part have been imposed by the fact that Marx was sharing two small rooms with a wife; three small children; Lenchen, their German maid; and presumably the odd visiting Prussian spy taking outraged notes about the scruffy bearded figure snoring contentedly on the sofa in mid-afternoon.

Despite this, Marx now set himself a tireless regime of research in the British Museum. The 1848 revolution had failed and a period of severe repression had set in over Europe, causing many radicals to despair. But Marx was equipped with exceptional psychological endurance. While biding his time he decided to work out his revolutionary ideas on paper, a task that would take him through the first long years of his isolation. Living in London, Marx was ideally situated for this task. In 1856 a superb new reading room opened at the British Museum, providing the finest research facilities in the world beneath a vast dome (whose Italian designer had ensured that it would not surpass the dome of St Peter's in Rome by covertly reducing its diameter by a few inches). Here Marx could study Hegel and Feuerbach in the original German and investigate in detail the works of Smith and Ricardo, as well as consulting the rows of bound parliamentary committee reports that lined the walls beside his favourite seat.

Marx quickly became a familiar figure about the streets of Soho. Even in the hirsute Victorian era, he stood out from the crowd – a fact only accentuated by his thick German accent, which he did nothing to improve. The diet of bread and potatoes, the cheap cheroots constantly staining and fumigating his beard and lungs, the sedentary life and heavy drinking – these soon began to take their toll. He began to suffer from painful boils: a curse of biblical proportions which continued to rack his flabby frame until the end of his days. But others in the family were not possessed of such stamina, and two more of his children died in infancy.

As if all this weren't bad enough, Marx also had an affair with the family maid, Lenchen Demuth, and made her pregnant. Engels, a frequent visitor, selflessly took the blame upon himself. When Lenchen was delivered of a small dark hirsute son, Jenny had her suspicions, but she kept these to herself for the sake of the family. Years later, on his deathbed, Engels revealed the truth to Marx's daughter Eleanor (known as 'Tussy').

Young Freddy Demuth would grow up to become a true member of the proletariat, working in an engineering factory in Hackney, in London's working-class East

End. In old age he would live to see the ideas of both his 'fathers' come to fruition in the Russian Revolution and the establishment of the Soviet Union. Freddy's siblings were less fortunate. Marx's oldest daughter, Laura, would commit joint suicide with her anarchist husband while living in poverty in Paris. His favourite, Tussy, chose the same path after being rejected by her philandering lover, who even gave her the prussic acid that she drank, causing her excruciating death.

Yet times were not unrelieved misery *chez* Marx. On sunny Sundays the family would travel up to Hampstead Heath for jolly picnics, with leapfrog and other party games afterwards. A farcical description remains of a drinking spree which Marx embarked upon with some German friends. This ended with a 'student prank' – smashing some gas lamps with stones, followed by a dash through the night streets to elude the chasing 'bobbies' (the slang name for the London police, so called after Sir Robert Peel, who had created the first uniformed London police force some two decades earlier). In temperament Marx remained very much the perennial student. As with the man, so with his ideas? This has always remained open to debate. Yet, as we shall see, no description of one would be complete without the other, such are their echoes, parallels, and dialectical contradictions.

From all accounts, sheer285 fecklessness was the main contributor to Marx's persistent poverty. Engels continued to send regular money, and Marx was even taken on as London correspondent of the *New York Daily Tribune*, at the time the world's biggest-circulation newspaper. He was contracted to write twice-weekly commentaries on British and Empire news, though these would frequently have to be dashed off by Engels in order to meet the deadline. Here too Marx honed his political technique. When the Indian Mutiny broke out, he was asked by his editor to predict its result, and wrote to Engels: 'It's possible that I shall make an ass of myself. But in that case one can always get out of it with a little dialectic. I have, of course, so worded my proposition as to be right either way.' (Thus began a Marxist tradition which would outlast the collapse of both the British and the Soviet empires.)

Despite Marx's regular income, his correspondence with Engels frequently included desperate pleas for more cash, citing the imminent arrival of the bailiffs, no food in the house, and such. He was completely open in discussing his political ideas with Engels, and this intimacy extended to his personal life – even going beyond financial emergencies to include such details as the eruption of a boil on his penis, or how he'd decided to take things easy and remain indoors because he'd pawned his only pair of trousers so he could buy cigars. Karl Marx or Groucho Marx? – it's sometimes difficult to tell. To quote some relevant economic statistics – in the manner that Marx himself so favoured in his works – he received £150 a year from Engels, as well as £2 for each of his biweekly articles for the *Tribune*. Even at his very lowest ebb, his annual income never dropped below £200, while the income for a clerk during this period was £75. Marx's expenses were modest: his annual rent for Dean Street was just £22, and Lenchen would have received £20 a year (had she ever been paid). Somehow the remaining £178 of Marx's income simply evaporated into the tobacco-clouded air while Marx sat sunning himself at the window in his underpants.

Despite their poverty the Marxes always had a maid. The long-suffering Lenchen had originally been a Rhineland peasant girl sent to look after them by Jenny's aristocratic parents. Regardless of their bohemian existence, Karl and Jenny appear to have retained certain pretensions. Marx remained steadfastly unwilling to stoop to actual labour, prefering to write at great length about the conditions of such activity. This prompted his exasperated mother to comment, 'What a shame little Karl doesn't make some capital, instead of just writing about it.' Meanwhile Jenny Marx still insisted upon using her inherited title, Baroness von Westphalen (a fact which was invariably overlooked in Soviet and Chinese biographies).

From Jenny's family the Marxes eventually received the small legacy that enabled them to escape from grim Dean Street and move to the more genteel suburban poverty of Grafton Terrace in north London. Despite his unwillingness to provide materially for his family, Marx remained a much-loved paterfamilias – referred to by one and all by his nickname 'Moor'. Visitors might find him on all fours giving 'elephant rides' as his children clung to his back, his hair, his beard, squealing with delight. During these years Marx allowed his hair and beard to grow longer and longer, assuming a consciously Promethean appearance. In his own eyes he was now 'writing the future'. Marx also seems to have found a (brief) solution to the problem of providing for his family. When Jenny received another small legacy, he wrote in a letter to a friend: 'I have, which will surprise you not a little, been speculating . . . especially in English stocks, which are . . . forced up to a quite unreasonable level and then, for the most part, collapse. In this way, I have made over £400 and . . . I shall begin all over again. It's a type of operation that makes small demands on one's time, and it's worthwhile running some risk in order to relieve the enemy of his money.' Since this is the only mention Marx makes of his new hobby, we can only assume that next time round it was not 'the enemy' who was relieved of his money. In any event, Marx now returned with renewed vigour to his radical dissection of capitalism.

By 1859 Marx had at last completed his first full-scale economic work, *Contribution to the Critique of Political Economy*. Marx's philosophy is based upon the following analysis: Social life is founded on economic life, upon how things are produced within a society. Social relations are based upon economic relations. Above these rises a corresponding superstructure of laws and social consciousness which reflects the economic structure. In this way the ideological and intellectual life of a society is entirely determined by the way things are produced within it. In Marx's words, which had already begun to generate their own lumpen jargon: 'The mode of production in material life determines the general character of the social, political, and intellectual processes of life. It is not the consciousness of men which determines their existence; it is on the contrary their social existence which determines their consciousness.' The echoes of Feuerbach and Stirner are still clearly discernible.

1859 also saw the publication of Darwin's *Origin of Species*. Ideas of evolution were very much in the air. Marx sketches a philosophical evolution of consciousness – which he sees as developing in a quasi-dialectical fashion rather than through the survival of the fittest. Originally we lived in harmony with nature (thesis). It was only by opposing nature that we realised ourselves as human beings (antithesis). Out of this struggle was born our consciousness (synthesis). Similarly, the further evolution of human consciousness has remained inseparable from struggle. But this evolution had now reached a stage where it was fatally blighted. In the interests of efficiency, economists had taken on board the notion of division of labour. Instead of each worker in a factory undertaking the complete production of each item, the manufacturing process was broken up into a number of specialised tasks. In the production of a wooden box, for instance, it was more efficient to have one worker sawing up the wood into planks, another sawing these planks into the required lengths, another assembling the requisite planks needed for the manufacture of a single box, another nailing these together, and a final worker varnishing the box. In this way, many more boxes could be produced than if each worker went through the entire process of making a box. But this more efficient process wreaked havoc on the morale of the workers themselves.

Marx saw this process as destructive of the consciousness of everyone involved. When workers were reduced to the continuous repetition of a single, mind-deadening task, they lost any meaningful relationship with the product they were helping to create.

Instead of being creative artisans, they became dehumanised drudges. Marx used the word *alienation* to describe this condition – another concept he derived from Hegel, who traced its historical development to Roman times. Alienation was the false 'unhappy consciousness' that was experienced among the downtrodden plebeians and slaves during the height of the Roman Empire. Previously they had experienced the harmonious social life of paganism, which had now been crushed. As a result, individuals turned their consciousness inwards, away from the misery of their actual reality, towards the transcendent, otherworldly kingdom of God. This was the dialectical process that had enabled the Christian religion to spread so quickly throughout the Roman Empire. Pagans had previously revelled in themselves and their world. Christians withdrew from the world and regarded their own lives as worthless. They became 'alienated' from themselves.

Marx characteristically downgrades the spirituality of Hegel's concept, seeing it entirely in economic terms. But it is worth pointing out that echoes of Hegel's dialectical concept could still be heard during the Industrial Revolution in Britain. A religious revival, much resembling the fervour of early Christianity, occurred among the alienated working class in industrialised Britain. Nonconformism and small Christian sects mushroomed in the working-class districts of British cities during this period.

Another crucial concept in Marx's economic philosophy was the concept of private property. This was essential to the entire process of market production. Objects were produced, sold and then owned. 'Private property has made us so stupid and partial that an object is only *ours* when we have it, when it exists for us as capital, or when it is directly eaten, drunk, worn, inhabited etc., in short *utilised* in some way . . . All the physical and intellectual senses have been replaced by . . . the sense of *having*.' Instead of satisfaction on an individual and communal level, all the worker received was money – literally and metaphorically, hard cash. In Marx's view, money had 'deprived the whole world, both the human world and nature, of their own proper value. Money is the alienated essence of man's work and existence; this essence dominates him and he worships it.' When the production and marketing of goods is motivated entirely by profit, social justice and even basic human needs are disregarded. Such an economic world, which finds its raison d'être solely in profit, results in grotesquely distorted social relationships which affect all human activity. Political, intellectual, artistic and even spiritual life all echo this method of production, which is justified by financial gain rather than any other form of social benefit. Seen in this light, history is transformed. Morality, the law, even religion do not evolve according to a history of their own. Such consciousness, both individual and social, is dictated by economics, by what Marx called historical materialism. Material existence dictates our consciousness, not vice versa.

The history of the twentieth century would show how Marx's answer to these problems went catastrophically wrong. Private property, money, the profit motive and alienation would seem to be fundamental to our present stage of evolution. We make use of them – as they make use of us. Alienation becomes heightened individuality. On the other hand, Marx's analysis reaches far beyond the early Victorian society to which it was applied. His description of money worship, our attitude to private property, consumerism, and the pursuit of profit for its own sake are all too relevant to the age of downsizing, provoked currency crises, rocketing technology stocks based on unreal values, and companies whose assets consist of everything except the people who work in them.

All this is analysed in much greater detail in Marx's massive masterwork, *Das Kapital* (*Capital*), the first volume of which he published in 1867. Alas, Marx's finest work is also his most unreadable. A typical sentence, chosen at random: 'The progress of accumulation lessens the relative magnitude of the variable part of capital, therefore, but this by no means excludes the possibility of a rise in its absolute magnitude.' The first volume continues like this for well over a thousand tightly packed pages – with two volumes to follow. It famously prompted the British prime minister Harold Wilson, who is generally recognised as having gained the finest economics degree ever at Oxford, to state flatly, 'I have never read Marx' – an astonishing if understandable omission. As an economic analyst, Marx is equalled only by Adam Smith and Keynes.

Das Kapital investigates the mechanisms of economics against the background of mid-nineteenth-century Britain. This was the most advanced industrial economy in the world and appeared to indicate the future. Both in capacity and efficiency, British industry far outstripped its competitors. An indication of the full extent of British supremacy is given by the following figures which Marx quoted with regard to the cotton industry. In England the average number of spindles per factory was 12,600, whereas its two main industrial rivals, France and Prussia, could manage only 1,500 spindles per factory. The full magnitude of this advantage becomes clear when we learn that the average number of spindles that could be maintained by one worker was 74 in Britain, but in Prussia just 37, and in France only 14. The cost of labour and the cost of the product were similarly affected.

Yet despite this vast supremacy, the British worker's conditions were appalling. A poor-law doctor in Bradford made a list (included in full in *Das Kapital*) which showed that his patients were living *on average* a dozen to a room, with some more than twice this. A street with more than two hundred houses was likely to have fewer than forty primitive outside lavatories. Those who lived under these conditions worked long and hard. A skilled factory hand in the north of Ireland was required to work from 6 a.m. until 11 p.m. from Monday till Friday, stopping at 6 p.m. on Saturdays. 'For this work I get 10s 6d [53p] a week', the worker explained to the visiting factory inspector. All the statistics that Marx collected were from the official reports in the British Museum: the capitalist system freely provided the evidence against itself (a suitably dialectic process).

Marx also pointed out that previous economic theory 'proceeds from the fact of private property. It does not explain it.' Private property was not a permanent feature, as any glance at history would show. In the beginning there had been tribal property; next ancient communal or state property; then feudal or estate property (conferring social 'status' on its owners); thence had come the bourgeois notion of private property. But what underlay all this social development? As we have seen, Marx viewed history as a succession of class struggles. In ancient society the slave class struggled against the freemen; later the Roman plebeians struggled against the patricians; then the serfs against 'their' lords, the mediaeval journeymen against the guild masters. 'Oppressor and oppressed stood in constant opposition to one another . . . an uninterrupted fight, now hidden, now open, a fight that each time ended either in a revolutionary reconstitution of society at large or in the common ruin of the contending classes.' Historical progress marched in a dialectical fashion. Each phase developed its own contradictions, which eventually resulted in the progressive synthesis of a new social system. Capitalism was simply another phase in this inevitable historic progress.

As capitalism developed, it too generated its own inherent contradictions. A free market led to an increase in competition. In order to increase efficiency and profits for his business, the bourgeois capitalist invested in machinery. Small businesses that couldn't afford such capital investment were driven to the wall. This intensifying competition led to larger and larger enterprises dominating the market, until eventually a monopoly was established. Hence competition led to the contradiction of a monopoly. At the same time the introduction of machinery meant increasing unemployment. But this served to diminish the market – the unemployed had no wages to spend on the greater numbers of goods being produced by this increased efficiency. More goods, declining market, decreasing profits. Thus further contradictions within the system emerged.

If, on the other hand, there was a boom which resulted in full employment, the workers' wages were bound to rise according to the law of supply and demand. There would be no pool of unemployed who could be drawn upon to work for lower wages. Higher wages would eat into profits. Either way, the capitalist's profits would inevitably dwindle. These internal pressures arose within capitalism as a result of its own development. The result was a series of recurrent and ever-deepening crises. These would eventually lead to the final crisis which would bring about the collapse of the capitalist system.

According to Marx, capitalism was basically unjust. It relied upon the exploitation of the workers, because the capitalists owned the means of production: the machinery, the tools, and so forth. A cotton bale arrived at the factory door, and left as garments which could be sold for a higher price. In this way the worker in the factory added value to the goods. But he was not paid the full value he had added. In fact, he was paid a subsistence wage, or little more; the factory owner pocketed the surplus value as profit. This, according to Marx, was exploitation.

Marx was a firm believer in the labour theory of value. A product had a *real* value which could be calculated according to the amount of labour that had gone into its production. When machinery entered the equation, it was valued according to the amount of labour that had gone into *its* production. Such a theory has all the appearance of justice. Unfortunately it is at odds with the circumstances in which it is applied – namely, the marketplace. The amount of labour used in making an article is highly likely to affect its price. One would expect a car to cost more than a bowl of rice; but in free trade the market is the *ultimate* arbiter. Supply and demand will always override labour cost. In the midst of a famine, a bowl of rice may even fetch more than a car.

Similarly, Marx's analysis of the manufacturing process severely misjudges the role of the capitalist. He risks his money when he sets up the enterprise in the first place, and for this he requires a reward to make his investment worthwhile. This is the driving force of capitalism: enterprise – imagination – risk. Economic motives are for the most part the acceptable face of avarice. No one embarks upon an enterprise if there is no possibility of gain and the only prospect is the risk of loss. Such is human nature. The domineering and exploitative behaviour of the capitalist class – the demonised 'bourgeoisie' – in Victorian Britain was often grotesque. Likewise their attitude to the hideous poverty they inflicted on the proletariat ('Good day to you, Mr Engels').

As history has shown, however, it was largely the people who ran the system, and the freedom they were allowed, rather than the system itself that was at fault. Unchecked power has always been a recipe for exploitation and hypocrisy. The capitalist system itself is only partly to blame. Capitalism seems to resemble Churchill's democracy: 'the worst form of government except all the other forms that have been tried'.

What was required to aid the victims of capitalism was government intervention rather than the radical alternative that Marx proposed. In his view, the balance of social and economic justice could only be redressed when the means of production were taken over by the state. Such forms of bourgeois private property should be nationalised. This is precisely what happened in the Soviet Union and throughout the Communist world. Free enterprise was stifled in favour of state planning: the Five-Year Plan, the Great Leap Forward, and the like. Under favourable conditions this may appear all very rational and just. But human evolution – either social or individual – has at best only aspired to reason and justice, rather than embodied these qualities. A controlled economy may attempt the occasional great leap forward, but it is unlikely to create a Silicon Valley. Such leaps spring from the intoxication of individual imagination rather than from sober committees.

Even so, elements of Marx's critique of capitalism still have relevance. Many of these elements we choose to ignore. We prefer our own 'working-class heroes' to the Stakhanovite versions depicted six times life-size bearing red banners in socialist realist murals. Yet the working-class heroes of contemporary capitalism only appear to have bucked the system. Our rock stars, sports millionaires, and whiz-kid floor traders still don't own the means of production. Here today, gone tomorrow – while the owners of the means of production continue to pocket any surplus value. (The film stars of Hollywood understood this as long ago as 1919, when Chaplin, Fairbanks and others created United Artists in order to own their own studios and control distribution.)

Marx felt certain that not all the contradictions that developed within capitalism were negative. The proletariat may have depended upon their wages for subsistence and been unable to accumulate savings or capital of their own. (This, for Marx, was the definition of the proletariat.) But in the factories of capitalism this perennially exploited class was developing into a skilled and disciplined labour force. As a class it would have a vital role to play in the next inevitable stage of historical dialecticism. When capitalism collapsed as a result of its own internal contradictions, there would be a revolution and the proletariat would take over the means of production. A 'dictatorship of the proletariat' would then be established. Marx follows this prediction with a characteristically dramatic pronouncement: 'With this social development the prehistory of society ends.'

Yet for Marx the dictatorship of the proletariat was only the first stage. This would be followed by a socialist utopia which very much resembled the woolly vision of Saint-Simon. The struggle between classes, which had been a permanent feature of 'prehistory', would be replaced by a classless society. The state would eventually 'wither away', the old market relations would disappear, money would be abolished, and everyone would receive his or her just desserts. 'From each according to his ability, to each according to his needs.' Apart from these few theoretical pointers, Marx had little to say about the actuality of his socialist utopia. Even Saint-Simon was more specific in his dream. But an outline of Marx's ideas, however brief, would not be complete without his quaint picture of the heaven on earth that would emerge out of the ruins of Stone Age capitalism:

'No one is limited to any single sphere of activity. Each individual can become accomplished in any activity he chooses. Society itself regulates the general production, and in this way makes it possible for me to take up one thing today and another tomorrow. I can hunt in the morning, fish in the afternoon, rear cattle in the evening [sic], and offer my own critical opinions after dinner. I can do all this, depending upon how I feel, without ever having to become a hunter, fisherman, herdsman, or critic.'

There is little need to expose the dialectical contradictions generated by this Dean Street pipe dream. Cows do not thrive under the attentions of whimsical part-time milkmen, especially in the dark. But more practical socialistic schemes *can* work in small communities of like-minded individuals: Israeli kibbutzes, Amish communities and similar efforts provide lasting evidence of this. Yet on the larger urban and state levels, society is evidently too complex. The dictatorship of the proletariat and the state appropriation of the means of production would lead in the twentieth century to a very different form of dictatorship from the temporary one that Marx envisaged. Far from withering away, the state expanded into an all-powerful monster, unchecked by competition or opposition.

What Marx had not realised was that capitalism's inner contradictions would play a large part in prompting it to evolve, rather than destroying it. Marx was not the only one to misjudge capitalism. None of the great thinkers of his era – from Mill to Nietzsche – had an inkling that capitalism would mushroom in quite the way it has. What Marx saw as the death throes of capitalism turned out to be little more than its birth pangs.

Karl Marx died in 1883 at the age of sixty-four. A dozen friends and fellow-believers gathered at the graveside on that cold March morning in Highgate cemetery. They listened as Engels delivered what must have seemed a hopelessly overblown funeral oration: 'His name and work will endure through the ages . . .' Less than seventy years later, a third of the world would claim to be run according to Marx's ideas.

AFTERWORD

Marx's great venture – communism – has now all but completely failed. Yet the force of its beliefs should not be forgotten. Marx's ideas offered the prospect of 'justice on this earth' to countless numbers who had never dreamed that such a thing might one day come. Quasi-Marxist ideas would be espoused, at least momentarily, by such twentieth-century luminaries as Einstein, Bertrand Russell, Wittgenstein, Tolstoy, Gandhi and Nelson Mandela. Many now claim that his ideas are of little contemporary relevance. In detail, his critique is said to apply only to the mid-nineteenth-century economy that he analysed (and not always correctly). But the larger picture has changed, and continues to change, in line with his key contention. Philosophy is not an island unto itself; it takes place within society, which is run on economic lines. Who is the economy for? How can its benefits best be shared in a just manner? Such questions remain very much alive. We are beginning a century where the division between the first and the third worlds continues to deepen, where even in the first world the division between rich and poor grows disruptively wide. And not only wealth will need to be rationed more appropriately, in a world whose resources themselves are approaching their limits.

Marx sought to control the market. The free market has survived, and will continue to do so, because it has not only learned how to evolve but how to control itself. This is why economics, for all its flaws and pretensions, becomes increasingly vital to our survival. The people who brought Seattle to a standstill during the first World Trade Organisation meeting of the new millennium were not for the most part Marxist extremists or the American poor. No matter their conduct, or the inchoate ideas they expressed: what drove them was a sense of injustice. Others in the world, powerless and less fortunate than the protesters, were getting a raw deal. As Marx in his own way showed, we ignore this fact at our peril.

FROM MARX'S WRITINGS

Philosophers have previously only interpreted the world, but the real task is to *change* it.

Theses on Feuerbach

Religion is simultaneously an expression of genuine suffering and a protest against this suffering. Religion is the sigh of oppressed creatures, it is feeling amidst a feelingless world, the soul of our soulless condition. It is the *opium* of the people.

Towards a Critique of Hegel's Philosophy of Right

To be radical is to grasp the root of the matter. But for the human being, the root of the matter is the human being himself.

Towards a Critique of Hegel's Philosophy of Right

A spectre is haunting Europe – the spectre of communism.

Opening words of the *Communist Manifesto*

The history of all hitherto existing society is the history of class struggles.

The freeman and the slave, patrician and plebeian, lord and serf, guild-master and journeyman – in a word, the oppressor and the oppressed, in constant opposition to one another, have carried on an uninterrupted, sometimes hidden, sometimes open conflict, a conflict that each time ended either in a revolutionary reconstitution of the entire society or the common ruin of the conflicting classes . . .

The modern bourgeois society which has sprung up from the ruins of feudal society has not done away with class conflicts. It has only established new classes, new conditions of oppression, new forms of conflict in place of the old ones.

Communist Manifesto

Instead of exploitation, veiled by religious and political illusions, [the bourgeoisie] has substituted naked, shameless, direct brutal exploitation.

The bourgeoisie has stripped the halo from every profession which was once honoured and admired with reverent awe. It has turned the doctor, the lawyer, the priest, the poet and the scientist into its paid wage-slaves.

The bourgeoisie has ripped the sentimental veil from family life, and reduced the family relation to a mere money-relation.

Communist Manifesto

The proletariat have nothing to lose but their chains. They have a world to win.

WORKERS OF THE WORLD, UNITE!

The call to arms at the end of the *Communist Manifesto*

The ultimate aim of this work is to reveal the economic law of motion of modern society.

Capital

Migrant labour is used for building and draining work, for brick-making, for lime-burning, railway-making, etc. This mobile column of disease brings smallpox, typhus, cholera and scarlet fever wherever it pitches camp. On projects involving a large outlay of capital, such as railways, etc., the contractor usually houses his labourers in wooden huts. These improvised villages lack all sanitary arrangements, are beyond the control of the local authorities, and are extremely profitable to the contractor. Here he manages to exploit his workers in two ways at once – as labourers and as tenants. Huts have one, two or three holes, and the navvies who inhabit them are charged a weekly rent of 2, 3 or 4 shillings accordingly.

Capital

And a rather more typical passage revealing Marx at his worst:

The value of the productive capital P is equal to C, the value of its formative contents, which in the stage M–C confronted the capitalist as commodities in the hands of their sellers. Secondly, however, the value of the yarn contains a surplus value of £78 = 1,560 lb. of yarn. Thus as the value expression of the 10,000 lb. of yarn, C = C + ΔC, C plus an increment (£78) which we shall call *c*, as it exists in the same commodity form as the original value now does.

Capital

From each according to his abilities, to each according to his needs.

Critique of the Gotha Program

The prophetic words of the poet Heine, written as early as 1842:

Little mentioned at the moment, communism is the dark hero lurking in hidden garrets on miserable straw pallets – the hero destined to play a great, even if only temporary, role in the modern tragedy. He is only waiting for the cue to make his entrance. We must never lose this actor from our sight . . . we must seek out the rehearsals where he prepares in secret for his debut.

History generally, and the history of revolutions in particular, is always richer in content, more varied, more many-sided, more lively and more 'subtle' than even the best parties and the most class-conscious vanguards of the most advanced classes imagine.

V.I. Lenin

Revolutions have never lightened the burden of tyranny: they have only shifted it to another shoulder.

George Bernard Shaw

CHRONOLOGY OF SIGNIFICANT PHILOSOPHICAL DATES

6th C BC	The beginning of Western philosophy with Thales of Miletus.
End of 6th C BC	Death of Pythagoras.
399 BC	Socrates sentenced to death in Athens.
c 387 BC	Plato founds the Academy in Athens, the first university.
335 BC	Aristotle founds the Lyceum in Athens, a rival school to the Academy.
AD 324	Emperor Constantine moves capital of Roman Empire to Byzantium.
AD 400	St Augustine writes his *Confessions*. Philosophy absorbed into Christian theology.
AD 410	Sack of Rome by Visigoths heralds opening of Dark Ages.
AD 529	Closure of Academy in Athens by Emperor Justinian marks end of Hellenic thought.
Mid-13th C	Thomas Aquinas writes his commentaries on Aristotle. Era of Scholasticism.

1453	Fall of Byzantium to Turks, end of Byzantine Empire.
1492	Columbus reaches America.
	Renaissance in Florence and revival of interest in Greek learning.
1543	Copernicus publishes *On the Revolution of the Celestial Orbs*, proving mathematically that the earth revolves around the sun.
1633	Galileo forced by church to recant heliocentric theory of the universe.
1641	Descartes publishes his *Meditations*, the start of modern philosophy.
1677	Death of Spinoza allows publication of his *Ethics*.
1687	Newton publishes *Principia*, introducing concept of gravity.
1689	Locke publishes *Essay Concerning Human Understanding*. Start of empiricism.
1710	Berkeley publishes *Principles of Human Knowledge*, advancing empiricism to new extremes.
1716	Death of Leibniz.
1739–1740	Hume publishes *Treatise of Human Nature*, taking empiricism to its logical limits.
1781	Kant, awakened from his 'dogmatic slumbers' by Hume, publishes *Critique of Pure Reason*. Great era of German metaphysics begins.

1807	Hegel publishes *The Phenomenology of Mind*, high point of German metaphysics.
1818	Schopenhauer publishes *The World as Will and Representation*, introducing Indian philosophy into German metaphysics.
1889	Nietzsche, having declared 'God is dead', succumbs to madness in Turin.
1921	Wittgenstein publishes *Tractatus Logico-Philosophicus*, claiming the 'final solution' to the problems of philosophy.
1920s	Vienna Circle propounds Logical Positivism.
1927	Heidegger publishes *Being and Time*, heralding split between analytical and Continental philosophy.
1943	Sartre publishes *Being and Nothingness*, advancing Heidegger's thought and instigating existentialism.
1953	Posthumous publication of Wittgenstein's *Philosophical Investigations*. High era of linguistic analysis.

CHRONOLOGY OF MARX'S LIFE AND TIMES

1818	Born 5 May at Trier in the German Rhineland.
1835	Enters Bonn University to study law.
1836	Leaves for University of Berlin to study philosophy.
1840	Friedrich Wilhelm IV becomes kaiser of Prussia, heralding a new era of reactionism. Left Hegelians dismissed from universities.
1841	Doctorate finally issued by University of Jena, but by now Marx's hope of an academic career has vanished.
1842	Appointed editor of *Rheinische Zeitung* (*Rhineland Times*). Engels becomes a Communist.
1843	Marx marries his childhood sweetheart, Jenny von Westphalen. Marx and his new bride depart for exile in Paris. Becomes editor of the *German-French Yearbook*.
1844	Marx begins his lifelong association and close friendship with Engels.

1845	*German-French Yearbook* closed down by French authorities. Marx expelled from France, takes up residence in Brussels, Belgium.
1848	Completes *Communist Manifesto*. Returns to Germany and becomes editor of *Neue Rheinische Zeitung*. 'Year of Revolutions' throughout Europe. Kaiser Friedrich Wilhelm IV dissolves Prussian Assembly and suspends democratic rights.
1849	Marx's protest ends in his arrest and trial; acquitted by sympathetic jury. Final 'red' edition of *Neue Rheinische Zeitung*. Banished from Germany. Marx and family arrive in London, which will remain his home for the rest of his life.
1850	Penniless Marx and family evicted from lodgings into the street. At the end of the year, moves to 28 Dean Street, Soho, ten minutes' walking distance from the British Museum, where he would do his research in the reading room.
1851	Great Exhibition held in London.
1852–1857	Employed as London correspondent of the *New York Daily Tribune*.
1856	Legacy left to Jenny enables Marx and family to move out of Soho to comparatively elegant Grafton Terrace in north London.
1861	Start of American Civil War.

1867	First edition of first volume of *Das Kapital* (*Capital*) published in Berlin.
1870	Outbreak of Franco-Prussian War.
1871	French defeat; Prussians occupy Paris. Paris Commune.
1872	Death of Marx's wife Jenny.
1873	*Das Kapital* fails to find an English publisher: no English translation of this work would appear during Marx's lifetime.
1880s	Marx's last years dogged by 'chronic mental depression'.
1881	Russian Tsar Alexander II assassinated.
1882	Writes preface to second Russian edition of *Das Kapital*.
1883	Marx dies.
1885	Publication of *Das Kapital*, volume 2 (edited by Engels).
1894	Publication of *Das Kapital*, volume 3 (edited by Engels), completing Marx's masterwork.
1917	Communist takeover in Russia.
1918	Short-lived Communist governments established in Bavaria (Germany) and Hungary.
1945–1950	Communist regimes established throughout Eastern Europe.
1949	Communists take power in China.
1989	Fall of Berlin Wall heralds collapse of communism throughout Europe and the Soviet Union.

RECOMMENDED READING

Terrell Carver, ed., *The Cambridge Companion to Marx* (Cambridge University Press, 1992). A selection of authoritative essays covering a wide range of Marx's thought, from his philosophy of history to deepest politics.

Eugene Kamenka, ed., *The Portable Karl Marx* (Viking, 1983). The best sampler of Marx's philosophical, political and economic ideas, containing well-chosen extracts from all the major works.

Karl Marx, *Das Kapital* (*Capital*) (Penguin, 1993). Marx's masterwork, which establishes him as one of the great economists of all time. Its prose is notoriously heavy going. Turn to the index and work your way in. By far the most interesting passages are those in which he quotes from government reports concerning working-class conditions in nineteenth-century Britain.

Karl Marx and Friedrich Engels, *The Communist Manifesto* (Signet, 1998). The best primer on Marx's idea of communism. A clear, succinct and stirring work which covers the philosophical, political and economic aspects of his thought.

Francis Wheen, *Karl Marx* (Norton, 2000). A lively and always entertaining retelling of the great man's heroic life and foibles. By far the best biography available.

Allen W. Wood, *Karl Marx* (Routledge, 1999). A full-scale critical work that concentrates on Marx's philosophy and its implications in other fields.

INDEX

alienation 29, 30–31

Berlin University 4, 9
Bonn University 4

capitalism 18, 27, 33, 34–38
Chartists 13
Christianity 7, 29
Communist League 15–16, 19, 21

Darwin, Charles; *Origin of Species* 28
Demuth, Freddy 23–24
Demuth, Lenchen 22, 23, 26

Einstein, Albert 40
Engels, Friedrich 13–16, 20–21, 24, 25, 39
  The Condition of the Working Class in England 13–14
epistemology 11–12

Feuerbach, Ludwig 6–7, 23, 27
Free Trade 17, 18, 33, 41

German-French Yearbook 13, 14, 15
God 6, 7

Hegel, Georg 4–8, 23, 29
Heine, Heinrich 3, 45

Kant, Immanuel 3
Keynes, John Maynard 31

Lenin, V.I. 45

Marx, Hirschel 3
Mill, John Stuart 38

Neue Rheinische Zeitung 19–20
New York Daily Tribune 24–25
Nietzsche, Friedrich Wilhelm 6, 38
Nonconformism 29

Owen, Robert 13

Prometheus 8–9
property 29–30, 31, 32

Rheinische Zeitung 9–10, 11, 14
Ricardo, David 11, 23
Russell, Bertrand 40

Saint-Simon, Comte de 37
Schumann, Clara 1
Shaw, George Bernard 46
Smith, Adam 11, 17, 23, 31
Spectator 21
Stirner, Max 8, 27

United Artists 36

Westphalen, Jenny von 10, 20, 26
Wilson, Harold 31
Wittgenstein, Ludwig 40
Works:
Communist Manifesto 1, 16–19, 42–44
Contribution to the Critique of Political Economy 27–31
Critique of the Gotha Program 45
Das Kapital 31–38, 44–45
Theses on Feuerbach 42
Towards a Critique of Hegel's Philosophy of Right 42

A NOTE ON THE AUTHOR

PAUL STRATHERN was educated at Trinity College, Dublin, and lectures in mathematics and philosophy at Kingston University. He has written five novels, one of which won a Somerset Maugham Prize. His most recent works include *Dr Strangelove's Game: A Brief History of Economic Genius* and *Mendeleyev's Dream: The Quest for the Elements*, which was shortlisted for the Aventis Science Prize. He has also written for many journals including the *Observer* (London), *Wall Street Journal* and *New Scientist*. His popular Philosophers in 90 Minutes series is being published worldwide in fifteen languages.